JACOB RIIS'S CAMERA

Bringing Light to
Tenement Children

Alexis O'Neill

Illustrated by
Gary Kelley

CALKINS CREEK
AN IMPRINT OF BOYDS MILLS & KANE
New York

I hate darkness and dirt anywhere, and naturally want to let in the light. . . . I love to mend and make crooked things straight.

—Jacob Riis

The power of fact is the mightiest lever of this or of any day.

—Jacob Riis

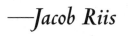

Twelve-year-old Jacob hated Rag Hall.

The rest of Ribe, Denmark, was filled with trim homes, sweet grass meadows, and fresh wind blowing from the sea.

But Rag Hall was a rat-infested, ramshackle dwelling.

As soon as he earned extra money, Jacob donated it to the poor in Rag Hall to help tidy things up.

Fifteen-year-old Jacob

had a mind of his own.
Although his schoolmaster
father expected him to become a
teacher, Jacob went to Copenhagen
and became a carpenter.

Twenty-one-year-old Jacob
was determined and persistent.

When the rich mill owner's daughter, Elisabeth, turned down his marriage proposal, Jacob sailed to America to earn his fortune and ask her again.

But when Jacob arrived in New York in 1870, he discovered that jobs for immigrants were hard to find, hard to keep.

Undaunted, Jacob scrambled to earn a living—carpenter, coal miner, mule driver, muskrat hunter, field hand, salesman, and more. He took lessons to learn how to operate a telegraph machine, but he ran out of money before he finished the course.

Often penniless, Jacob slept in abandoned barns, fields and cemeteries, and in homeless shelters that were so filthy and disease-ridden, he vowed to put an end to them someday.

One winter evening, Jacob sank down
on some steps,

weak with hunger,
destitute,
homesick for Denmark,
lovesick over Elisabeth,
and utterly alone.

As luck would have it, the principal
of his telegraph school walked by. Jacob
explained his plight. The principal knew
Jacob to be a bright young fellow, so he
gave Jacob a note recommending him for
a reporter's job at the New York News
Association.

To Jacob, reporting was a noble calling. Back in Denmark, Jacob had helped his father edit a newspaper. He admired how reporters made people's lives better through their stories.

Before long, Jacob landed a job at the *South Brooklyn News*. He saw

pushcart vendors being robbed,
children laboring in sweatshops,
homeless boys begging on the streets.

Day after day, Jacob learned the business—first as a reporter, then as editor, and finally as owner of the newspaper.

And through all this, his love for Elisabeth still burned.

At last, Elisabeth agreed to marry him. Jacob sold
the newspaper to pay for his voyage to Denmark for the
wedding, and he and Elisabeth moved to New York. When
their first son was about to be born, Jacob knew he needed
to earn enough to support his growing family.

Jacob landed a job as a police reporter, chasing down
crime stories for the *New York Tribune* for the princely sum of
twenty-five dollars a week. And his life began to change.

Jacob's office sat a few blocks from Mulberry Bend, New York City's worst slum, and right across from police headquarters. He often worked until two or even four o'clock in the morning. Then he would put on his hat, adjust his spectacles, and walk the whole foul length of Mulberry Street, through Bandit's Roost, Bottle Alley, Baxter Street Alley, Ragpickers Row,

across Five Points,
and down to Fulton Ferry
on his way home to Brooklyn.

What Jacob saw in those neighborhoods gripped his heart:

tenement buildings obscuring the skies,
apartments jammed with immigrants—
   Slavs, Italians, Jews, Irish, Chinese,
families toiling in stifling sweatshops,
the stench of mold and kerosene choking the air,
privies overflowing in courtyards,
children without green places to play.

Jacob wrote vivid articles about life in the tenements. Yet his words failed to ignite change. The appalling conditions did not improve.

If only Jacob could *show* others what he saw in the slums—rooms packed with people, rooms dark both day and night. How could he shine light into these places?

Then one day, Jacob found the answer . . .

Blitzlicht, a special flash powder!

When photographers ignited the powder, dark places lit up brightly.

Perfect!

To get accurate, truthful images, he would photograph the tenants. And he needed to capture them at night, when the rooms were crowded.

He asked two amateur photographer friends to help him.

One midnight, the men hauled heavy equipment up pitch-dark, narrow tenement staircases. They flung doors open and fired.

Boom! Click.

Blinding light! Smoke everywhere!

Next room.

Boom! Click.

Terrified tenants bolted through the windows. They dashed down fire escapes.

He captured them—with a camera.

When his friends tired of the late-night hours, Jacob bought a small four-by-five-inch wooden box camera.

He practiced taking pictures.
He practiced using flash powder.
Twice, he set fire to dwellings.
Once, he even set fire to himself.
But he didn't give up.

When Jacob reported illegal, extreme overcrowding . . . *fifteen adults and a week-old baby sleeping in a room meant for four people—and there wasn't even a bed!* . . . the Board of Health ignored him.

Furious, he carried images—still dripping from the darkroom—to the board. Look! See them? The board paid attention.

That's the solution! Words and photographs *together. This* was the way to show people the truth.

For his ground-breaking presentation, Jacob projected life-sized photographs with a stereopticon as he delivered a passionate, story-rich lecture about the children and families in the tenements. This tour of the slums opened the eyes of church groups, missions, and charity groups to the plight of the city's poor who lived in squalor.

In 1890, Jacob's words and photographs were published as a book, *How the Other Half Lives*.

The book grabbed readers' hearts.

His book also grabbed the attention of the newly appointed president of the Police Board, Theodore Roosevelt.

Roosevelt left a card on Jacob's desk that said, "I have read your book, and I have come to help."

In Roosevelt, Jacob found a kindred spirit. At night, they walked the streets of Mulberry Bend together. Both expressed outrage at the conditions they saw. Both were incensed at the treatment of the poor. Both burned to

provide safe shelters for the homeless,
eradicate unhealthy, unlivable slums,
create clean, green parks and school playgrounds for the
  city's children.

Jacob inspired Roosevelt.
Roosevelt promised to use his power to make changes.
And he did.

Ten years later—
Filthy homeless shelters? Gone.
Bandit's Roost? Gone.
Bottle Alley, Baxter Street Alley, Ragpickers Row?
Gone, gone, gone.

In place of these slums, Mulberry Bend Park opened.
A place for children and families. A place

flooded with sunlight,
feathered with soft green grass,
bubbling with children playing.

In the end, Jacob Riis, who delved into social issues
at the age of twelve, spent his life bringing light into
dark places.

He did it with his camera,
with his words,
with his tenacity,
and with his belief in doing what was right.
But mostly, he did it with his heart.

And because of him, the lives of tenement children
and their families changed for the better.

It takes a lot of telling to make a city know when it is doing wrong.

—Jacob Riis

AUTHOR'S NOTES

Jacob the Immigrant and the Immigrant Experience

Like many immigrants before him, Jacob Riis chose to leave his country of birth (Denmark) and move to America, where he hoped he could earn a good living. Tens of thousands of immigrants arrived in New York, the major port of entry. Earning a living and finding a place to live proved more difficult than they expected. They lived in old houses intended for single families, which were broken up into several apartments, and in new tenements built for six to eight families but housed two or three times that number. In 1884, three quarters of New Yorkers lived in overcrowded buildings without adequate light, heat, or running water. Most believed that they could move to better conditions once they saved enough money. For ten years, Riis fought to condemn Mulberry Bend, a particularly wretched slum within blocks of his reporter's office. After ten years, he won the fight, and Mulberry Bend Park (now Columbus Park) gave residents outdoor space to relax and play. However, those who had lived in the Mulberry Bend tenements were faced with finding housing on their own in other parts of the city.

Jacob and the Progressive Era

During the Progressive Era (1890–1920), many individuals and organizations took action to change laws on child labor, women's suffrage, public health, substandard housing, school conditions, and more. Jacob's book *How the Other Half Lives* was a national bestseller and made him famous. He toured the country giving passionate lectures illustrated with his dramatic photographs, which helped convince more and more people that something had to be done. Tirelessly, until he died in 1914, Jacob told the story of the slums. He wrote dozens of magazine articles and several more books to become his generation's face and voice of reform. Housing reform, important to Jacob, was a complex issue that continues to be a major challenge in cities today.

Jacob's Family

Jacob and his wife Elisabeth (Gjørtz) moved from Brooklyn to Richmond Hill on Long Island, where they raised five children: Edward, Clara, John, Katherine, and Roger William. Jacob commuted by train and ferry to his job on Mulberry Street in New York City. His commitment to fill the tenement districts with parks—safe places outdoors where all children could play and enjoy nature—had an impact on his own children. One day, they gathered armfuls of daisies from fields by their home and gave them to Jacob to take to "the poors" in the city. He did, and encouraged others to do the same.

Our Family, Richmond Hill, Summer 1898

Jacob took this photograph of his family in the yard of their home in Richmond Hill, Long Island (now Queens), New York. Elisabeth, whom Jacob called "Lammet," sits in the center. Roger William, Clara, and Edward stand, and Katherine and John gather at her feet.

Jacob and Theodore Roosevelt

Jacob and Theodore Roosevelt had a lifelong friendship. Both men had big personalities, lots of energy, and a passion for fairness and justice and bettering the lives of children. As a team, they pushed for reforms that changed the dreadful Mulberry Bend forever. During Roosevelt's presidency (1901–1909), Jacob was a frequent visitor to the White House.

Jacob's Camera

Jacob never considered himself a photographer. "I had use for it, and beyond that I never went. I am downright sorry to confess here that I am no good at all as a photographer, for I would like to be. . . . I am clumsy, and impatient of details." The first flash photographs of the slums were taken at Jacob's request by Dr. Henry G. Piffard, Richard Hoe Lawrence, and Dr. John T. Nagle, while accompanied by Jacob and a policeman or two. Later, Jacob took them himself. After Elisabeth died, Jacob married Mary Phillips and in 1911 bought a farm in Barre, Massachusetts. Although he meticulously saved papers, letters, and journals, he left 412 glass negatives, 161 lantern slides, and 193 photographic prints behind in the attic in his Richmond Hill home. In the 1940s, photographer Alexander Alland Sr. found and saved these images just before a wrecking ball destroyed the home.

GLOSSARY

Blitzlicht: flash powder made of a mixture of magnesium powder and potassium chlorate used by photographers to illuminate dark locations

homeless shelter: public lodging for the homeless in New York City at the time was in the dirty basements or backyards of police stations, where each individual slept on a wooden plank

privy: an outhouse

reformer: a person who works to change and improve social or political conditions

stereopticon: a type of slide projector with two lanterns positioned so that one slide image appears to dissolve into the other

tenement: a narrow apartment building, usually about five to seven stories tall on a lot about twenty-five feet wide and one hundred feet long, that is poorly lit, poorly ventilated, and lacking indoor plumbing

TIMELINE

1849 Born Jacob August Riis on May 3 in Ribe, Denmark; one of fourteen children

1870 Sails to America on the *Iowa*, May 18

1870–1873 Works at various jobs; experiences homelessness

1873 Lands a job with New York News Association

1874 Becomes reporter, then editor, for the *South Brooklyn News*

1875 Buys the *South Brooklyn News*

1876 Marries Elisabeth Gjørtz, March 5, and returns to New York

1877 First son, Edward, is born, followed by Clara (1879), John (1882), Katherine (1887), and Roger Williams (1894)

1877 Becomes a police reporter for the *New York Tribune* with an office on Mulberry Street, across from police headquarters

1884 Inspired by Tenement House Commission meeting to report on reforms; builds a home at 524 North Beech Street in Richmond Hill, Long Island, and moves his family there

1885 Becomes US citizen

1887 First flash photographs of slums taken

1888–1892 Uses a single lens four-by-five-inch camera for images

1888 Delivers first illustrated lecture about the slums on January 25; experiments with flash powder; shows first photographic images of tenement interiors on February 28

1889 Publishes article "How the Other Half Lives: Studies Among the Tenements" in *Scribner's Magazine*, December, with illustrations based on his photographs

1890 Becomes a reporter for the *New York Evening Sun*; publishes book *How the Other Half Lives: Studies Among the Tenements of New York* with Charles Scribner's Sons, November; book includes his photographs printed in halftone

1892 Publishes book *The Children of the Poor* with Charles Scribner's Sons, October

1894 City government condemns Mulberry Bend tenements and promises to build a park in their place

1895 Theodore Roosevelt becomes New York City police commissioner, May 6

1896 Roosevelt abolishes police lodging houses

1897 Mulberry Bend Park officially opens, June 15; currently called Columbus Park in lower Manhattan

1899 Resigns from newspaper work; tours country giving lectures

1901 Publishes autobiography *The Making of an American* with the Macmillan Company; Theodore Roosevelt becomes president of the United States

1902–1914 Continues to tour the country giving lectures

1905 Elisabeth dies

1907 Riis marries Mary Phillips

1914 Jacob A. Riis dies, May 26 in Barre, Massachusetts

WHAT JACOB ACCOMPLISHED

From the obituary of Jacob A. Riis (1849–1914) in the *Hartford Times*, May 27, 1914:

Jacob A. Riis. He compelled the remedy of the filth and depravity in the old New York
    police stations.

He forced the construction of more school houses.

He exposed the contamination of the New York City's water supply and brought about the
    purchase of the whole Croton watershed.

He forced the destruction of the rear tenements, thus relieving the hideous darkness and density of
    life among New York's pitifully poor.

He brought about the obliteration of Mulberry Bend.

He made little parks to spring up in the dingy and crowded and unhappy places of New York.

He induced Police Commissioner Roosevelt to abolish the police lodging houses.

He drove the bakeshops out of the tenement basements.

He secured playgrounds for the schools.

He fought child labor.

He secured a truant school.

He wrote of the plight of the poor so movingly that he made even practical business men
    stop and think.

He spent his whole life in the service of his fellowmen. The service was successful.

He died poor.

That was the record of Jacob A. Riis. Seldom is America privileged to benefit by one so fine.

Peddler Who Slept in the Cellar of 11 Ludlow Street
    This peddler in the Jewish quarter slept on a mattress on planks suspended on barrels over water. Jacob described the scene: "It was an awful place, and by the light of my candle the three [peddlers], with their unkempt beards and hair and sallow faces, looked more like hideous ghosts than living men. Yet they had slept there among and upon decaying fruit and wreckage of all sorts . . . for over three years."

Sweatshop in Hester Street

One Sunday, Jacob toured the sweatshops of the Jewish quarter with a Yiddish-speaking guide. After he took this flash photograph, he described the room in which eight people worked: "The floor is littered ankle-deep with half-sewn garments . . . The faces, hands and arms to the elbows of everyone in the room are black with the color of the cloth on which they are working."

SELECTED SOURCES*

All quotations in the book can be found in the following sources marked with an asterisk.

BOOKS

Alland, Sr., Alexander. *Jacob A. Riis: Photographer & Citizen*. New York: Aperture Foundation, Inc., 1973, 1993.

Anbinder, Tyler. *Five Points: The 19th-Century New York City Neighborhood That Invented Tap Dance, Stole Elections, and Became the World's Most Notorious Slum*. New York: A Plume Book/Penguin Putnam, 2002.

*Riis, Jacob A. *How the Other Half Lives: Studies Among the Tenements of New York*. New York: Charles Scribner's Sons, 1890.

————. *The Battle with the Slum*. New York: The Macmillan Company, 1902.

*————. *The Children of the Poor*. New York: Charles Scribner's Sons, 1892.

*————. *The Making of an American*. New York: The Macmillan Company, 1901.

Roosevelt, Theodore. *Theodore Roosevelt, an Autobiography*. New York: Macmillan, 1919.

Steffens, Lincoln. *The Autobiography of Lincoln Steffens*. New York: Harcourt Brace, 1931.

Ware, Louise. *Jacob A. Riis: Police Reporter, Reformer, Useful Citizen*. New York: D. Appleton-Century Company, Inc., 1938.

Yochelson, Bonnie. *Jacob A. Riis: Revealing New York's Other Half—A Complete Catalogue of His Photographs*. New Haven: Yale University Press, 2015.

Yochelson, Bonnie, and Daniel Czitrom. *Rediscovering Jacob Riis: Exposure Journalism and Photography in Turn-of-the-Century New York*. Chicago: University of Chicago Press, 2007.

WEBSITES*

"Jacob A. Riis Photographs." Museum of the City of New York. Jacob A. Riis Collection encompasses more than 1,000 photos and is the sole archive of Riis's images. https://collections.mcny.org/Explore/Highlights/Jacob%20A.%20Riis/

"Past Exhibition: Jacob A. Riis—Revealing New York's Other Half." Museum of the City of New York. Lesson plans for grades 2–12. mcny.org/lesson-plans/past-exhibition-jacob-riis

Tenement Museum. Built on Manhattan's Lower East Side in 1863, this tenement apartment building was home to nearly 7,000 working class immigrants. tenement.org/

* Websites active at time of publication

The Baby's Playground

A toddler stands on a dirt-strewn floor in a dark tenement hallway in front of a broken sink at the top of a staircase, its bannister held in place with rope. Jacob ironically called this dangerous place, "a baby's playground."

VIDEOS

"A Layman's Sermon: Jacob Riis on How the Other Half Lives and Dies in New York." Recreation of Riis's traveling lecture, with a voiceover derived directly from a script he wrote matched with images he actually used. youtube.com/watch?v=K3NwFB9zuF8

"Light." *How We Got to Now with Steven Johnson*. PBS.org. Oct. 29, 2014. Demonstration of flash photography techniques used by Jacob Riis. youtube.com/watch?v=H6Yo7Ivd63E

"New York City Video: Jacob Riis." Recreation of Jacob Riis's lecture and use of the flash revolver in capturing tenement-dweller photographs. history.com/shows/america-the-story-of-us/videos/jacob-riis

"10 Homes That Changed America: 4: The Tenement Mid-19th Century." *WTTW Chicago Public Media*. A tour of a Lower East Side tenement at 97 Orchard Street, New York, NY. interactive.wttw.com/ten/homes/watch/#.VwUcHPkrKM (scroll down and click on segment #4 The Tenement)

"Five Cents a Spot"

Jacob described this room lit by a kerosene lamp: "In a room not thirteen feet either way slept twelve men and women, two or three in bunks set in a sort of alcove, the rest on the floor." The owner of this illegal boarding house charged homeless people "five cents a spot" for the night instead of seven cents, the minimum for a hammock or cot required by law.

I have found the only safe plan to be to stick to the truth and let the house come down if it must. It will come down anyhow.

—Jacob Riis

Bandit's Roost

Bandit's Roost at 59 ½ Mulberry Street was one of the dark back alleys of Mulberry Bend torn down to make way for Mulberry Bend Park. One of Riis's first photographs, it shows Italian mothers and children living alongside young gangsters.

FURTHER EXPLORATION

BOOKS FOR YOUNG READERS

Bial, Raymond. *Tenement: Immigrant Life on the Lower East Side*. Boston: HMH Books for Young Readers, 2002.

Freedman, Russell. *Immigrant Kids*. Logan, IA: Perfection Learning, 1995.

Freedman, Russell. *Kids at Work: Lewis Hine and the Crusade Against Child Labor*. New York: Clarion Books, 1994.

Hopkinson, Deborah. *Shutting Out the Sky: Life in the Tenements of New York, 1880–1924*. London: Orchard Books, 2003.

Manning, Maurie J. *Laundry Day*. New York: Clarion Books, 2012.

Markel, Michelle. *Brave Girl: Clara and the Shirtwaist Makers' Strike of 1909*. Illustrated by Melissa Sweet. New York: Balzer + Bray, 2013.

Pascal, Janet B. *Jacob Riis: Reporter and Reformer*. Oxford: Oxford University Press, 2005.

I hate darkness and dirt anywhere, and naturally want to let in the light . . . I love to mend and make crooked things straight.

—Jacob Riis

In memory of Frances Patrick "Frank" Murphy Jr. of Syracuse, New York.
Friend, photographer, independent scholar. —AO

In memory of Joseph Solman; immigrant, NYC East Village artist.
Long time inspiration who opened his studio to me. —GK

ACKNOWLEDGMENTS

With thanks to Bonnie Yochelson, Art Historian and former Curator of Prints and Photographs at the Museum
of the City of New York; Daniel Czitrom, PhD, Professor of History, Mt. Holyoke College; Carl Ballenas
and Helen Day of the Richmond Hill Historical Society and Friends of the Maple Grove Cemetery; Margaret
Marshall and Lucy Allen of the Barre Historical Society; and Museum of the City of New York. Also thanks to
Gretchen Woelfle, Julie Frankel Koch, and Angelica Carpenter.

PICTURE CREDITS

Richard Hoe Lawrence and Henry G. (Henry Granger) Piffard (1842–1910) for Jacob A. (Jacob August) Riis (1849–1914) /
Museum of the City of New York. 90.13.4.104: 46

Library of Congress, Prints and Photographs Division: LC-DIG-ggbain-05687: 39; LC-DIG-ds-07174: 40; LC-
USZ62-12492: 42; LC-USZ62-23305: 43; LC-USZ62-25663: 44; LC-USZ62-16348: 45

Calkins Creek
An Imprint of Boyds Mills & Kane
calkinscreekbooks.com
Printed in China

ISBN: 978-1-62979-866-0
Library of Congress Control Number: 2019939441

First edition
10 9 8 7 6 5 4 3 2 1

The text is set in Centaur MT Std.
The illustrations are done with etching ink and pastel on paper.